The Superpower Foods: Protein, Fat, and Carbohydrates

Did you know your food has **powers**?

It helps you grow **strong**, hour by hour!

Three big helpers you need on your plate,

Protein, fat, and carbohydrates!

Protein builds your muscles **strong**,

It keeps your bones **healthy** all along.

Eggs, chicken, beans, and yogurt too,

These **superfoods** work hard for you!

Salmon
Yoghurt
Cheese
Tofu
Eggs
Beef
Chicken
Edamame
Beans

To lift, to jump, to grow and play,

Protein helps you every day!

Fats help your body feel **full** and bright,

They give you the energy to **play** just right.

Avocados, nuts, and seeds—you'll see,

Fats help you thrive and be

the best you can be!

Avocado
Seeds
Butter
Coconut
Olives
Olive oil
Nuts

Rice
Apples
Carrots
Bread
Corn
Potatoes
Pasta
Bananas
Berries
Broccoli
Sweet potatoes
Lentils

Carbohydrates help you run and play,

Fueling your body throughout the day!

Oats, sweet potatoes, and bananas too,

Helping you jump, learn,

and **power** through!

When proteins, fats, and

carbohydrates combine,

You'll feel amazing, **strong**, and fine!

Like eggs with toast and avocado too,

Or yogurt with seeds and berries

— just for you!

YUM!

These foods together help you **grow**,

A **balanced meal** gives you a steady flow!

Vegetables and fruit have something more,

Fiber and vitamins you'll adore!

Fiber fills you up and keeps **hunger** away,

Vitamins fight **colds** and keep

sickness at bay!

Peppers, apples, carrots, and greens,

A rainbow of colors for **growing machines!**

Try them all, and you will see,

Healthy and happy is the way to be!

yay!

When you're eating, here's what's right,

Listen to your **tummy**, it's your best guide!

If you feel **full**, then you've had enough,

You don't have to finish, it's not that tough.

And if your tummy feels **hungry** once more,

You can always ask for a little bit **more!**

Now, let's repeat what we have learnt!

Protein helps your body grow strong,

Fats give you fuel to keep moving along.

Carbohydrates power your body to play,

Together, they help you feel great!

So when you eat, just remember this way,

Protein, fat, and carbohydrates

power your day!

Parent's Guide: *Encouraging Healthy Eating in Children*

As a parent, there's always so much to juggle — time, energy, and budgets often feel stretched thin. Making nutritious food choices can feel challenging, but even small adjustments can make a big difference. Here are some practical (and hopefully enjoyable) ways to nurture a positive relationship with food for the whole family.

Cook together

Cooking together is a wonderful way to explore food, connect, and build valuable skills. It's an opportunity to talk about the size, shape, colour, texture, and smell of different foods, as well as to learn about numbers and fractions, food chains, and other subjects — all while making lasting memories. When children are involved in preparing and handling food, they're often more excited to try it. Child-friendly tools, like safe knives and peelers, help children practice their skills safely and build confidence in the kitchen.

Share meals as a family

Eating together and sharing the same meal creates positive experiences around food. Family meals make trying new foods feel more comfortable and enjoyable.

Give foods and meals silly names

Soup can become "Dinosaur stew", Bananas - "Monkey snacks", and Cauliflower can transform into "Cloud puffs". Make up meal names accordingly, create little family traditions around these meals, and rotate them weekly.

Encourage self-serving

Allow children to serve themselves, even with small scoops. Self-serving encourages independence and helps them feel in control of what they put on their plates, making them more open to new foods.

Choose whole foods

When you can, opt for minimally processed ingredients like proteins, vegetables, grains, and fruits. Whole foods provide natural flavours and nutrients, helping kids develop a taste for healthy choices.

Offer new foods with a favourite food

When introducing a new food, pair it with something your child already enjoys. This makes the meal feel safe and familiar, reducing resistance to trying something different.

Offer small portions of new foods repeatedly

Research shows that children may need to see a food multiple times (sometimes 10–15!) before feeling comfortable trying it. Start with very small portions of new foods, alongside familiar favourites, so they don't feel overwhelmed.

Offer toppings and condiments

Let kids personalise their meals by adding their own toppings like cheese sprinkles, yogurt dips, or silly faces made with chopped veggies.

Serve a variety of foods without commenting

Offering a range of foods without commenting on their taste or nutritional value keeps the experience neutral. Let kids discover flavours on their own, without added pressure or expectations.

Practice patience and praise effort, not just outcomes

If you feel like it, acknowledge small steps, like touching, smelling, or licking a new food. Praise the effort ("You tried it!") instead of the result (like finishing the food), so they feel encouraged to explore further. For example, you could say "You had a bite of broccoli. Broccoli are green and look like mini trees, don't they."

Encourage mindful eating

Help kids recognise hunger and fullness cues, letting them know it's okay to stop when full or ask for seconds if hungry.

Enjoy sweet foods mindfully

The topic of sweet foods can be a sensitive one for many families. Decades of misleading information, combined with the overwhelming availability of sugary options in stores—such as cakes, cookies, pastries, ice cream, candy, chocolate, and much more—make it difficult to navigate. Refined sugar and sweeteners also hide in unexpected items like bread, sauces, condiments, ready meals, and juices, further complicating the picture. Deep cultural traditions around sweet foods add to the challenge.

Research shows that regularly consuming high-sugar foods and drinks can affect children's appetite, focus, gut microbiome, and overall physical and mental health. When possible, make sweet foods at home, using less refined sugar. If buying these items from a store, choose those with simple, recognisable ingredients, and avoid products with long ingredient lists or additives such as emulsifiers, sweeteners, and "natural flavourings" if you can.

Avoid uing food as a reward or punishment

Using food as a reward or punishment can create an unhealthy relationship with eating. Instead, focus on teaching children that food is meant to nourish and enjoy, not to control behavior. By removing emotions like guilt or reward from eating, you help your child develop a balanced and positive approach to food.

Celebrate achievements and handle challenges in ways that don't involve food—for example, through quality time, words of encouragement, or fun activities together.

Try These Games For Better Mealtimes

These engaging games and activities transform any moment into an opportunity for kids to explore new foods. From blindfold taste tests to creating colourful rainbows on their plates, these playful approaches encourage children to engage with new flavours and textures.

"Food Bingo"

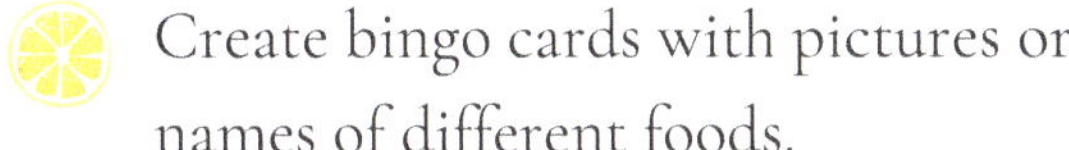 Create bingo cards with pictures or names of different foods.

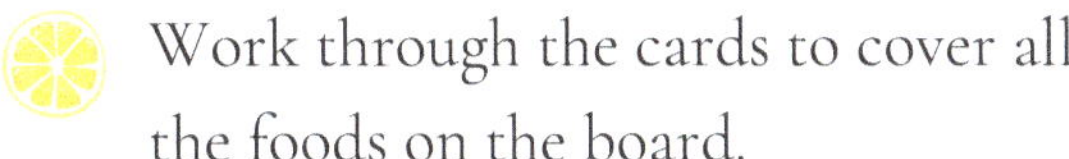 Work through the cards to cover all the foods on the board.

The first one to get bingo is the winner.

"Guess the Flavour" Blindfold Test

Place small bites of different foods (both familiar and new) on a plate.

Blindfold your child and ask them to guess each food they taste.

You can take turns to make it more fun.

"Restaurant Night" at Home

Work with your child to design a special menu with new dishes and old favourites.

Put on your aprons and cook the meal together!

Set the table, let your child be the customer, and you be the server.

Apple Tasting Adventure

Sample and compare different apple (or other fruit) varieties, discovering new favourites.

Rate each apple on sweetness, tartness, and more!

Learn fun facts about the different types of apples.

"Build a Rainbow" on Your Plate

 Challenge your child to create a rainbow with their food.

 Provide a variety of colourful fruits and vegetables and let them arrange them on their plate to make a rainbow.

 Talk about the different colours and nutrients in each food.

"Grow Your Own Food"

 Involve your child in growing their own fruits, vegetables, or herbs.

 Plant herbs like basil or chives, or try fast-growing veggies like radishes, and watch them flourish!

 This can help them develop an appreciation for where food comes from and make them more interested in trying new things.

"I Spy" Food Edition

 Play a game of "I Spy" using foods in the kitchen or on the plate.

 For example, "I spy something red and juicy" (a tomato).

 This game builds familiarity with different foods and keeps kids engaged.

"Build-a-Snack"

 Give your child foods they can assemble themselves, like crackers, cheese, and fruit slices.

 Let them "build" mini sandwiches or towers.

 This hands-on play with food helps develop fine motor skills and makes snack time more interactive.

You're already doing so much to care for your child, and helping them build healthy habits is just one part of the journey. Small, thoughtful steps add up over time. Your effort, no matter how big or small, is making a difference—and that's something to celebrate. Be kind to yourself and enjoy the process; you're doing an amazing job!

For more information, printables such as food colouring books, flashcards, activity sheets, and much more, visit:

<u>www.braindropsbooks.com</u>